NERVE

STORM

Also by Amy Gerstler

The True Bride

Primitive Man

Past Lives

Bitter Angel

Nerve Storm

Amy Gerstler

PENGUIN POETS

PENGUIN BOOKS
Published by the Penguin Group
Penguin Books USA Inc., 375 Hudson Street,
New York, New York 10014, U.S.A.
Penguin Books Ltd, 27 Wrights Lane,
London W8 5TZ, England
Penguin Books Australia Ltd, Ringwood,
Victoria, Australia
Penguin Books Canada Ltd, 10 Alcorn Avenue,
Toronto, Ontario, Canada M4V 3B2
Penguin Books (N.Z.) Ltd, 182–190 Wairau Road,
Auckland 10, New Zealand

Penguin Books Ltd, Registered Offices:
Harmondsworth, Middlesex, England

First published in Penguin Books 1993

1 2 3 4 5 6 7 8 9 10

Page ix constitutes an extension of this copyright page.

LIBRARY OF CONGRESS CATALOGING IN PUBLICATION DATA
Gerstler, Amy.
Nerve storm / Amy Gerstler.
p. cm.
ISBN 0 14 05.8703 9
I. Title.
PS3557.E735N47 1993
811'.54—dc20 93-14681

Printed in the United States of America
Set in Goudy Old Style
Designed by Cheryl L. Cipriani

for Benjamin Weissman

Thanks to the following people for their invaluable assistance:

Dennis Cooper, Sid and Mimi Gerstler, Will Gillham,
Michelle Huneven, Alexis Smith, David Trinidad,
Benjamin Weissman and Megan Williams.

ACKNOWLEDGMENTS

The following poems in this collection were previously published, some in slightly different form:

"Overheard on the Soul Train," "That Calm Sunday That Rolls On and On," "Losing Heart," and "Sad Women's Harvest Song" in *Brooklyn Review*; "Ether," "Lost in the Forest," and "On Wanting to Grow Horns" in *Witness*; "Mr. Right" in *Urbanus and Raizirr*; "Freud's Apology," "Grass," and "Duet" in the catalog for the exhibit "Helter Skelter," published by MOCA, the Museum of Contemporary Art, Los Angeles; "Dust" in *Indiana Review*; "Extended Vacation" in *St. Mark's Poetry Project Newsletter*; "Around the Block in Eighty Days" in *Special Issue*; "Suffering in the Old Testament" in *Framework*; "The Mermaid's Purse" in *Michigan Quarterly Review*; "A Sinking Feeling," "Dead Hunters," "Duration," and "An Invalid" in *The American Poetry Review*; "Diary of a Lonely Antcatcher" in *Now Time*; "Daughter of Eve" and "Modern Madonnas" in GAS; "The Stretcher-bearers" in *Bastard Review*; "The One for Me" in *Santa Monica Review*; and "Consolation" in *Denver Quarterly*.

"On Wanting to Grow Horns" also appeared in *Best American Poetry 1992*, Charles Simic and David Lehman, editors, published by Scribner's.

Extracts from "Diary of a Lonely Antcatcher" appeared in a limited edition artist's book in collaboration with Judie Bamber, published by Jonathan Hammer.

CONTENTS

NERVE

STORM

PETITION

That slightly curdled
ration of morning milk,
handed to you in a dented
tin cup: that was me.
You hardly knew who
you were swallowing,
though it seems I've
always been with you.
In yet another life,
I found myself sprouting
fuzzy leaves, a tufted shrub
inclined toward a beam
of artificial light
in your hothouse.
Next century, I materialized
as the well-timed squirt
of lime juice
trickled between your lips
by a fellow sailor to keep
you free from scurvy.
Generations later, I stood
on a rocky shore,
dressed as a woman,
and watched you drown—
sucked out by a particularly
vicious undertow.
(Not one of my incarnations
has been able to swim.)
You lay flat on your back
on the beach, pebbles
stuck to your palms,

profile waxy and swollen
under someone's yellow
raincoat, salt water running
from your mouth and nose.
Another time, in a green,
succulent country,
I leaned down to kiss you
and was bucked off my horse.
You remind me of the scent
inside my mother's cedar-lined
walk-in closet, where I
often found myself confined
for various unrepented
childhood crimes.
The cedar's reek
was almost religious,
an orchestral smell—
like an antique cello's
dissonant memoirs. O pursuer
fused to the pursued,
changing sex and shape
throughout the ages,
masquerading as a weather vane
or border guard, a jailbird
or radio wave: we, the undersigned
patiently wait to be reborn;
this time, we hope,
as that chalky substance
that coats your tongue,
or as your white nightgown.

SHROUD SONG

This is one sweet nothing
whispered into a dear
corpse's ear: You'll never
escape my embrace.
I was your winding sheet,
a mindless starched garment,
the dispirited skin you groped
toward when you grew too ill
and asked to be excused.
I concentrated on translating you
accurately, beautifully, into
the ancient picture language
of gravy stains. I served as
your personal cotton sanctuary,
attentive as breath,
sopping with modesty.
Waking up wrapped in fabric
is better than waking up
in a stork's smelly nest
imbued with cyanotic blue,
back at your bloody, blurred,
difficult beginning. Isn't it?
The subdued misty tint
of an overcast morning
obscures you, as you recede,
becoming less than the sum
of your parts: a chemical
treasure trove. Air, water
and fire equitably, quietly
divide you up between them.

Scarlet fever

Since you desire to know
the origin of the heart
murmur which restricts
my activity and marooned
me on this spit of land
that became the windswept
island of my life,
leaving me to stew in my own
weak, unseasoned juices—
I transmit the following
lengthy telepathic message,
which finds you tonight
in the silence of your study,
drinking tonic and cataloging
medicinal plants: *Baby Jade,
Balsam Root, Chalice Vine,
Bishop's Weed,* plus that fungus,
whose name I can never remember,
you saw mentioned in an old text
describing orgies taking place after
celebrants chewed a few of the butter-
colored mushrooms.

So . . . I caught scarlet fever
from a glass of tainted milk
at age eight, just when my braids
had reached the desired length
and I could finally sit on the tips.
The milk tasted weird,
but I was crouched behind a hedge

4

watching a couple (both of whom
were married to other people)
kiss, not in the tight-lipped
dry way my parents smooched,
but with their mouths wide
open, like aquarium fish.
Fascinated, I kept drinking it in.
At first flush of sickness, I felt
something flex and take aim;
a hot, heavenly, inflected breath
exhaled, bull's-eye, right in my face.
A few mornings later, my cereal
turned to sawdust. Normally
fragrant tea smelled like gasoline.
My mother told me to quit being silly.
People at school were encircled
by fiery lines of light.
My thoughts crackled with static.
The roots of my hair throbbed.
I was sent home from Spanish class,
nearly delirious, with a nasty note,
one line of which read: "We
assume you have no wish to start
an epidemic." During the ensuing
three months I almost died
of abject loneliness.
Accustomed to having my every
utterance treasured, now whatever
I blew my nose or wiped my eyes
on was wrapped in plastic bags
and whisked out of the house,

as though what leaked from me
was obscene. What a pitiful
existence! How dark it was then!
My tongue looked like
an overripe strawberry—
bright red, tastebuds inflamed,
ready to germinate. My throat
got so sore I could only swallow
aspirin if it was pulverized
and sprinkled into juice.
When my rash faded, I peeled.
Flat on my back, miserable,
molting, I threw a tin of mints
at my mother's head one afternoon
when she sweetly asked me to try
not to scratch my itchy skin raw.
The only family member who remained
in my deteriorating good graces
was the dog, who lay on my bed,
shaking it occasionally
with her panting. She ignored
my feverish meanness
and spent her days lovingly
licking my empty slippers.

An uncle who lived
in another city, wore
suspenders and was
missing the end of one
pinky sent a present

to amuse me while I was
bedridden: a book
the size of my pillow.
I overheard my parents
discussing whether
to allow me to keep it
because it wasn't
a children's book,
and so possibly
"not suitable" for me.
"*Extinct Birds*," my mother
muttered, "such a depressing
title for a sick child,"
so I wanted it, badly.
I got them to hand it over
by refusing to eat. Two
and a half missed meals,
and it was mine.

What was so transporting
about this particular volume?
Perhaps the fact that these
creatures could continue
to live only within
the confines of a book
made our predicaments feel
similar. It would improve
my lot, I decided, to become a loon
that shed tears, to live on lizards
and soft fruit. My nearly unhoused

spirit seemed composed of members
of some waning avian colony, anyway—
perpetually airborne, hesitant
to alight, afraid to swallow water,
to sleep, to complete migration.
A certain breed of bird "formed
great attachments to everyone
who was kind to them" and thus
the trusting species was easily
wiped out. Others, who lost
the power of flight, disappeared,
their dried feet prized by natural-
history museums. I shut my eyes
and wondered if my parents
would sell my hacked-off feet
to the Smithsonian after I died,
to display in a glass case.
I lifted the covers and peered
down at what museum-goers would
see: pale uneven toenails
instead of beautiful claws.

You, who think you love and know
me, so many drizzly decades
later, bent over your samples
of *Wild Carrot* and *Bermudagrass*,
tell me: What excuse can I make
for the way I turned out?
Why didn't I ever emerge from under
the canopy of those dripping

bird-laden branches into
some sort of clearing? Why am I
still trapped back there,
dimly flipping pages?

French leave

to the memory of Tim Dlugos

To remember your older
brother's bloodstained
mattress, pajamas
and bedding being burned
in the backyard
in the middle of winter—
but to recall this
only subconsciously,
and to sleepwalk
because of it.
To lie awake.
To have a fit
of the shudders
in public. To lose
the ability to speak
for a few minutes.
To be warmed by random
bursts of anger.
To hear someone crying
or having sex in the next room
in a remote desert motel.
To cover one's ears.
To observe the kitchen
curtains fluttering oddly
one breezeless evening
and wonder whose spirit
is visiting this time.
To half hope it's Tim,
who spoke so energetically

about Charles Dickens
from his hospital bed.
To call Tim's bravery
and limber eloquence
to mind, his late
pendulum swing
toward religion,
left open-ended
at the time of his swift
physical conversion.
To say to the waving
curtains (a white eyelet
Tim might have liked),
"What a beautiful form
your soul has taken,"
and to watch them
go instantly limp.

OVERHEARD ON THE SOUL TRAIN

—Having enough to eat or breathe is no longer an issue.

—Don't we get white dresses?

—I was the world's most beautiful baby and now I guess I will stay that way.

—I loved it when he choked and bit me!

—Animals liked me. I hope that counts for something.

—He would tell me he loved me while he had his hand down my sister's pants, but I believed him.

—Papa and I are speaking again after so many years!

—I owe my brother a punch in the stomach.

—Ah, monotony. Mired in silence, how I squandered my time.

—Mother said I ruined every family gathering I ever attended.

—I thought if I drank the bottle of solvent, I'd finally forget him.

—I just wanted to sleep hard for a long time.

—Being alive was a fruitless inebriation.

—I don't want anyone else wearing my pale blue seersucker suit.

—I was pressured into making a false confession.

—No one besides me seems to notice that in these trees flickering by the steamed-up windows, hummingbirds are turning into vipers, and vice versa.

—My psychiatrist kept saying I should force myself to eat.

—Nothing stayed in my impoverished body for long.

—They said it was only a flesh wound, but I died en route to the hospital anyway.

—I binged on dust, flirted with searchlights, and here I am.

—How long do I have to wear this ball and chain?

—A victory of light has been declared right between my eyes.

ETHER

You sleep when they decree,
on a litter of mumbled numbers
and a rubbery head-filling smell:
this feathered word *Ether*.
Each whiff's one nail
in a spiky bed
you levitate inches above—
a weightless guru
or long-suffering mist,
a wisp of cirrus separated
from his fellow clouds.
You're a balloon that breathes.

Nurses. Surgeons.
Masked bandits who'll
ghostwrite you. Gloved,
in green gowns redolent
of anesthesia's leaky history,
they drag you into the light,
turning you inside out,
as Mother did
with your best dresses
before tossing them
into the wash.
As you evaporate
they trade dark looks.
Insomniacs hate snorers.
Something in you breaks off,
flutters up and lodges just
under the white tile ceiling.

Rest cure

Five fingerlike paths
extend down to the lake
from the hotel. Its dim
frosty windows peer out
across ski-scarred snow,
their precise squareness
at a loss to understand
the long, drawn-out
sweetness of a frozen
field crunching underfoot.

I am forty years old,
she tells herself,
and do not understand
one blessed thing
that has happened to me.

The heavy drifts
on the roof, and two
dark rows of windows,
turn the hotel into
a white-haired head
with blackened teeth.
She sips from a pocket
flask, liquor brewed
in the neighboring
village from
caraway seeds.

. . .

Steps have been cut
into the icy hillside.
She walks carefully,
as though down a paneled
hall, lined with paintings
she has been warned
not to jostle—eight
generations of portraits
of unhappy ancestors,
thin nervous men
in pince-nez
and mustaches, whose
surname, roughly translated,
means "bird with small
spotted tail"; and big women,
their fat hands resting
on tables or in ample
pleated laps.

It's the first day
of the new year.
The lake isn't wholly
frozen. The barely
moving water's
slightly oily.
Its shifting colors
and textures
seem haphazard,
and at the same time,

significant,
a confession trying
to emerge from the
depths; a black mouth
full of swirling
iridescent globs,
about to form
its first words.

I would have been
an unfit mother,
she tells herself.

A heron picks its way
among stiff reeds,
stabbing the water for
frogs. How must it feel
to be skewered like that,
not through the heart,
necessarily, but some
expendable appendage,
a foot or a hand.
Richer, more astonishing,
certainly, than sitting
politely at the jeweler's
having your ears pierced.

How infants show too
much of the whites

of their eyes. The wet
enticement of kissing.
A bee drowned
in a cup of tea.
What do one's observations
sum to? A hodgepodge
of details; a cigar-box
collection of coins,
seashells, erotic paper
dolls. Patches of ice,
like psoriasis, make
the lake's surface scaly.
Luckily, she has always
had good skin.

She thinks she will ask
the local doctor for
a stronger prescription.
She remembers how it felt
to submit to his rational
and grumpy touch,
like her father's.
Her breaths rise
and hang in the air,
weightless as wreaths
of cream.

MR. RIGHT

Above all, I admire the man
who never quite materializes,
who wears his evaporation
like a hopelessly baggy jacket.
His hair and nails are made
not of protein, but apocrypha.
Where can I find such a model
citizen? Amidst the murky dregs
of my medicinal green tea
whose main ingredient appears
to be dried locust wings?
Will I know him only
as a musty archival smell
faintly perceptible
between the pages
of this biography
of a sixteenth-century pickpocket?
Or will he manifest his presence
in the perspiration
pressed onto my palm during
the bone-crushing handshake
of an otherwise rather
shadowy sort of man—
a tweedy, knock-kneed professor
of logic and ethics, whose
breath smells like bookbinding
glue? The mind bathes itself
daily in chemical tirades
till it grows lazy, vague,
and quits. Before that happens,
I want to tiptoe beneath

the threshold of human notice,
and prick up my ears
to invisibility's welcoming,
mosquitolike whine. I'll
learn to heed effacement's
disquieting advice. Then,
maybe I'll find him.

My place in his heart

An empty archive, my place in his heart's
an ill-lit ventricle whose walls heave
like the walls of a gasping man's chest.
This cell's low ceiling is dark soft-palate
pink. Giant photos of dead legends
autographed with cryptic endearments
serve as decor and as oracle:
they must tell our whole story.
I curl up on the floor in a corner
and watch dust motes mate as best they can.
Past blunders echo. Thuds and barks
sound the first bars of a rousing anthem
for the newly exhumed, my lullaby for tonight.
The tune's praised in braille
by tiny myopic stars who blink fiercely
and X-ray the earth at the same time,
reading its molten innards like soothsayers
or distant clinicians, but keeping mum
about what they learn.

THAT CALM SUNDAY THAT ROLLS ON AND ON

What the planets behold remains unheard of on earth.
That deadpan overview's lost to us, or sublimated
so deeply it's as good as forgotten—like the design
of ancient aqueducts, the ability to sniff
out water, or the art of raising the dead.
We read and weep less and less.
Is it winter again, so quickly? Gesundheit!
Is that a cold, or something a bit
more opportunistic? A virus with teeth.
Defacing the fruited plain seems to be
humans' favorite mode of self-expression lately,
a way of making sure we really exist,
letting the unruly landscape know who's boss.
Drifting off to sleep with as many lights as possible
left blazing delights us. OK. Here's some paper.
Would you rather be writing a last letter, alone;
or lose that final blinding moment wrapping Christmas
presents with your family? Wherever I lay my head
is home these days, just like you. So I guess
the end's best spent arbitrarily. While seas boil over,
stars burst, and angels do their flaming nosedives
I'd just as soon pass that long, awkward moment
with my head lolling in your lap,
listening to your bowels sing.

FREUD'S APOLOGY

Gentlemen, and the ever-present spirits of ladies,
whose sympathies I seek, deposit your secrets with me:
those sights, whispers and reeks that ruined you.
The voice of the giantess as she stood looming
in the nursery doorway—so like the whine
of a bloated queen bee. Zoo animals with ballooning
genitals. The diaper pin that pricked and goaded you
into a thicket of sexual splinters. Strict Papa
from whom you earned your pitiful allowance
with unorthodox grovelings. Dreams of oil stoves
and olive pits, of riding schools and ringworm.
That milky stain left by some forbidden confection
which caused you to doubt your origins. These obscure
hurts must be aired. Not enough has been written
about longings that alter the hairline, move you
to flirt with your kin or to contemplate life
as the sort of hyphen that occurs when a word
must be unceremoniously split between syllables.
Such fertile seeds need spilling. Who knows
what proud, erect breed of beanstalk
might sprout from them, or what manner
of psychic landscape I could reach
by climbing it, hand over hand, until,
engulfed by your foggy dreads
I am swallowed by them entirely.

A HYPOCHONDRIAC'S ACCOUNT
OF HERSELF

I've been clutching this sweet
little bottle of pills
for almost two hours
wondering whether I ought
to actually swallow one.

I shake one of the little devils
out onto my palm. So tiny,
but they wreak such havoc. Pills
act like nuclear bombs. They change
the landscape so drastically,
both without and within.

I think I have a canker sore.
My head throbs above one eye.
A spot right by my liver
pings. I have a pain
in my lower back the exact size
and shape of a butterfly. My bowels
have probably backed up into my brain
by now. What does this mean?
Where will it all lead?

What I remember most from childhood
is the walk to school. I hurried past
the local paper factory one time
when I was about eleven, almost
late for my first class again.

One of the grimy workers that hung
around the front gate slapped me
on the bottom and laughed, "Hey,
little sister, what's your rush?"
I ran the rest of the way to school
and almost missed my first period.
When I asked my friend Sara why
a man I didn't know would spank me
as I walked by, she shook
her head sadly and said
we'd meet after school
and she'd explain everything.

I remember wanting a dog so badly
when I was six, seven, eight years
old, but being told they were filthy
beasts, that I must never touch
their fur and if one happened to lick
me, to tell Mother right away, and she'd
scrub me with that sticky green liquid
disinfectant. (Time to be a big girl,
place two pills at the back of my throat,
and try not to gag before I can wash
them down with a swig of iced tea.)

Last week I went to a palm reader.
The doctor and that bald pharmacist
won't take my calls anymore. They let
their slutty receptionist keep me

on hold forever. The palmist greeted
me in a dingy storefront, next to
a movie theater that shows mostly
gay films. Her baby cried in a playpen
in the only other room—separated
from us by a wrinkled green sheet,
flapping in the doorway, meant
to serve as curtains. The infant
was just learning to stand,
wavering, pulling itself
to its feet using the bars
of the pen. I have never drunk
a drop of alcohol in my life.
I never smoked a cigarette.
Why should I always feel ill?
(Suddenly I am horribly hungry.)
The palmist said, "You will never
be troubled about money, but you
may have difficulty attaining
happiness." She didn't charge
much.

For some reason I dreamed about
parking my car on the sidewalk
that night. For some reason,
I awoke seeing double. For some
unfathomable reason, what I
picture most vividly
nine times out of ten
when I shut my eyes,

is the continuous arrival
of all those trains, filled
with prisoners, which I could
easily see from the windows
of my parents' front parlor.
O, but this was in another country,
not ours. Guards shouted and divided
the men into groups. Pity
has a definite aftertaste,
like when you lick the head
of a hammer—an iron flavor.
The prisoners' ribs stuck out
like railroad ties.
I could sense the purity
of their terrified intentions
through the glass, as though
they gave off radiation.
I felt someone stroking my cheek
as I watched them, though no one
was visibly near. Something about
them was the same as me,
but I never learned what those
binding similarities were,
and my parents would only say,
"*What* trains?" in a way that
told me I'd better drop the subject.
It seemed terribly important
that not a soul find out
how I might resemble those men,
but I did wish to know myself.
They spoke a crumbly-sounding

language that seemed designed
for humble renunciation.
(Since I don't feel any calmer,
I'll swallow another one.)

Often, in the evenings, my parents
threw parties. At one, after supper,
my father's business partner drew me
into a corner and said, "Why
you're such a bite-sized little
thing. I could just eat you up."
I murmured, "Then why don't you
try?" We slipped into the study.
I saw and touched all parts
of his body while he babbled
on and on about the wonderful
handiwork of God. This seemed
odd, because earlier, pontificating
at the table, he'd said we were
living in a time in which religion
had become useless and dull. We
committed, I suppose, several sins
of the tongue. Years and several
prophets later, an occasion
arose when another man, who bore
more than a slight resemblance
to the first, told me his heart
just wasn't in it anymore, while
I toyed with a bit of crystallized
ginger in a big, cut-glass dish

of preserved fruit the management
had sent up to our room. I told
myself at that moment his heart,
a bloody, aging mess, might be
the furthest thing from my mind,
among all the interesting things
beating, leaping, molting and
whirring on the pungent earth.
(I think my friends the little
blue pills are finally starting
to kick in.)

My muse

His filament-thin smile
is the type often seen
on the lips of an infant
with a full bladder, or gas.
Or, his smirk can resemble
the jerky, erratic line
of an electrocardiogram,
sketched in between
the nose and chin
of a young mother
who's just learned
she's got heart
trouble. This muse
never received proper
dental care when young.
Consequently, some of his
teeth have "jumped ship"—
his quaint phrase.
Unforgiving as blisters,
he's as wretched
as the skinny magician's
assistant he invented
to weigh on my mind.
She lies quietly
in her false coffin,
only her head and feet
visible. She tries
to relax while her tuxedoed
boss, a sweaty, uncertain
man who doesn't know chalk
from cheese, proceeds
to saw her in half.

DUST

Lightest of burdens,
it sifts over window
sills, entering open mouths
and noses of silly buildings.
It tumbles from the folds
of a never-worn dress
discovered in some attic.
Fuzz of nothingness
in time it becomes fur
to protect objects' tender
hides. Victor in all wars.
Gray obliterator.
The granite head
of a grimacing king
dwindles to this,
as flesh and stone meet
at dust's bone-dry crossroads.
Ageless buffer
composed of worlds
of enticing tininess,
orbiting in shafts
of sudden, misguided light,
looping the loop
with carnival exuberance.
Its mute grist is the exhaustion
of form. Dignified, it remains
the bane of housekeepers,
nemesis of the asthmatic
and the fastidious. It does not
respond to cross-examination.
Who is resigned enough

to give herself up to this?
Submit to the conqueror's
mortar and pestle, wear its cloak
of motes, be ground down to earth's
finest flour, which sprinkles
itself liberally over the ends
of all roads. Scattered by sneezes,
lens-clouder, most lusterless
of snows, you are substance's goal,
the be-all and end-all of
parchment, skin, dandruff, pearls,
crisp insect shells.
You're matter's last stop,
neglect's obscure handwriting,
desiccated beverage of ghosts.
You're action's fallout,
blurrer of ancient library titles.
As your lightless particles implode
they constantly mock their younger
siblings, the dim frivolous stars.

Extended vacation

Driving away, we pass a road sign
that reads POSSIBLE DUST CLOUDS.
The dumbfounded sense of probability
left ringing in our ears sounds like
a choir gargling milk. Soon, tussles
in the roadside shrubbery stir up
the promised dust. We also see tufts
of hair bound in sheaves—a harvest
of blame lugged in from the fields
by hired Gypsies. Acres of grapes
riddled with blight whizz by. How
can you feel anything at all for me?
I'm a haughty ailment, an ill-fated
crusade. I agree only to rubies.
I'll whine till you lift the skirt
of our flimsy agreement with the tip
of your cobra-headed cane, seeking
what's underneath. I lie down
in the ritual position till the debt
of flesh is collected. The dying person
forgives everyone, and she is always me.
You must perform several labors
before you may touch me. *Blunder, yearn.*
Love my mother. Capture that dust cloud
and give me a sponge bath with it.

Around the block in eighty days

This manual has been written
to help prepare you
for a breathtaking adventure.
It will explain how to locate
alternative sources of water
at gas stations and restaurants
whose lavatories are perpetually
locked, how to distinguish
wild rhubarb and prickly pear
from less delectable weeds
that force their way up
through cracks in the sidewalk,
as well as which beetles
are edible, in case you become
separated from the group.
Skills such as the ability
to quote the New Testament
while looking suitably humiliated,
or turn newspapers into a quilt,
provide a solid foundation
on which to build the confidence
that you can remain alive anywhere
on the block if you keep your wits.

You won't soon forget this block
you've washed up on like flotsam—
its bookstores and laundromats,
automated teller machines
and pharmacies that dispense
mostly aging bottles of nail polish.

Visit nomad encampments. Watch
public scribes write letters
for the growing illiterate.
Journey through miles of passages
hollowed out of solid rock
that lead to a secret underground
carwash. See the giant prehistoric
fish skeleton now used as a prison,
hear its ribs creak and groan.
Shed your hopes while sheltering
in architecturally significant
doorways, as birds doff their pin
feathers, as immigrants at Ellis
Island divested themselves
of syllables of surname,
so they might have an offering
for that statue with the spiked
crown, our Mother of Exiles.
One by one, they heaped those
beautiful unstrung consonants
right beside the broken chain
seldom seen at her feet.

Suffering in the Old Testament

In those days, there were no Committees to Defend the Unjustly Prosecuted. We were simply imprisoned by one mud wall of grief after another. New words and images were added to the list of blasphemies each day. Our sorrows, scrawled in giant ashen hand-writing, were common as graffiti, indelible as stains wrung from the dung and plant juice used in cave paintings—pagan artifacts, some of which we destroyed. In this, our earlier life, the jugular clarity of lightning announced god's verdicts. Men didn't judge other men because we knew we were still too stupid. New constellations blazed with a terrible light. God often appeared to future Moslems and Jews as a toxic swamp gas that overcame careless bathers. As typhus and cholera composed themselves, there were worse plague days when all sound vanished, and with it, all warnings. Even crows, those black accurate harbingers, were deprived of their tongues, and our wind chimes flapped and tangled mute as laundry, predicting silent storms. The world was young and benumbed enough to seem a plan in constant danger of being scrapped. Mumbling rivers could turn to sour milk or urine overnight. Divine forgiveness was a grace you had to kill and burn a fat goat to obtain. This was the beginning of bloodshed and waste as forms of worship, customs which prevail today. Trees could sweat and groan then, and when the ax flash split the air, we waited in the tainted silence that followed to see whose neck it would sever. Then we waited for other words to thunder into being, which we could use later to mull things over, comfort or defend ourselves. There were ghosts but they were never free to speak, so we learned nothing from them. Fugitives hid in wells. Our perpetual scattering began. The patterns certain women's footsteps left in sand spelled out lascivious messages, so we killed them. Is there anyone alive who remembers such a dark, uncivilized time? Only camels and asses.

THE MERMAID'S PURSE

Ours is the blue planet.
Not the hot bloody red one,
nor that pickled quagmire greenie
pitted with gulfs of nothingness,
but the mountain-wrinkled earth
covered with a little brush
and immense amounts of water,
most of which, as you know,
is inhabited by mermaids.
One afternoon you are walking
along the shoreline, sunburned,
sandy and salty-skinned,
when you notice a kind of container
you've never seen before. With its
texture of wet breadcrumbs
and nice pattern of webbing,
it can only be a mermaid's purse
washed up on the beach.
Cautiously, you pour its contents
out on the ground.
A boiling and hissing,
a flexible sizzling gumbo
is suddenly bubbling at your feet.
A couple of dogs lope over
and start nuzzling the mermaid's
stuff. How are you going to clean
it all up? The elegant, burrowing
anemone and the frilled
but nonetheless leathery
sea cucumber are otherwise
engaged. They're pretty busy.

So they can't help you.
Hey, what's that nameless mermaid
got packed in here, anyway?
A detached baby's ear
severed by kidnappers and tossed
off the pier, which was snatched
up by the responsible mollusks.
A swatch of thatched barnacle tatting.
A beautiful bleeding tooth
and a handful of pink buttons.
A double dose of soft soap
wrapped in green-tongued
gulfweed. A solitary paper,
upon which beach fleas practice
standing in a complicated
formation resembling the type
on page eighty of a Henry James novel.
A yellow-edged cake urchin
in case she gets hungry.
A particularly willful bit
of coral called a *reed starlet*
and her intellectual boyfriend
known as the *smooth brain*.
A kitten's paw to keep
the baby's ear company.
A sea peach and a peanut worm
in case she's asked to make salad.
A scotch bonnet, a red-bearded nipple
shrimp, a feather duster plus a
flashlight fish for emergencies.
You dig deeper into the purse

to find her rough girdle and veil,
as well as many *bent-nosed,*
soft-shelled, saw-toothed,
flame-streaked, shield-backed,
friendly, fuzzy, flattened, crimson,
ringed, greedy, lunar, mottled,
black-eyed, giant, horned,
tapered, speckled, blue-handed,
horn-mouthed, feathery, flare-nostriled
and *silvery* creatures all of whom
like you immediately
and want to know everything about you.
What you want to know is:
Does every mermaid carry
this much in her purse?
And if so . . . how can the oceans
swallow so much color
and remain so terrifically blue?

LOST IN THE FOREST

I'd given up hope. Hadn't eaten in three
days. Resigned to being wolf meat . . .
when, unbelievably, I found myself in
a clearing. Two goats with bells
round their necks stared at me:
their pupils like coin slots
in piggy banks. I could have gotten
the truth out of those two,
if goats spoke. I saw leeks
and radishes planted in rows;
wash billowing on a clothesline . . .
and the innocuous-looking cottage
in the woods with its lapping tongue
of a welcome mat slurped me in.

In the kitchen, a woman so old her sex
is barely discernible pours a glass
of fraudulent milk. I'm so hungry
my hand shakes. But what is this liquid?
"Drink up, sweetheart," she says,
and as I wipe the white mustache
off with the back of my hand:
"Atta girl." Have I stumbled
into the clutches of St. Somebody?
Who can tell. "You'll find I prevail here
in my own little kingdom," she says as
she leads me upstairs—her bony grip
on my arm a proclamation of ownership,
as though I've always been hers.

A SINKING FEELING

One feels like an animal
pacing its filthy cave.
Bits of bone litter the floor.
The rusty smell of turning meat
festoons the stagnant air.
One begins to think all action
leads to grief. Joints stiffen.
Arthritis prefigures rigor mortis.
The light is silver this late
in the year, razorlike, expedient,
on the verge of turning,
like that meat mentioned earlier.
Animals are happy on days like today.
Blessings melt down upon postmodern
heads, copious as flocks
of white-winged religious tracts
fluttering south for the winter,
illustrated with watercolors
of adults, children and dogs greeting
dead friends in the afterlife.
How could anybody be glum
in this superlative weather? Well,
I'll tell you. The day is a young
bubble, with a tiny fire at its core.
My four brothers and I were accidentally
shrunk to the size of ants this afternoon
by our bumbling garage-inventor daddy.
Now we're trapped inside the bubble
as it rises, weaving, on Dad's breaths
and mischievous breezes, floating toward
that open window. Bye.

On wanting to grow horns

for Tom Knechtel

Man's envy of animals is ancient,
a damp cave filled to the rafters
with handsome pallid bats, lemurs,
beetles, mallards. *Do I really
have to walk upright all the time?*
Swooping lucidly, melancholy enters
the mind through one's nasal
passages, like the homey smell
of burnt pot roast. Male fruit bats
court females by honking and flashing
tufts of fur on their shoulders:
not such strange behavior. Less
comprehensibly, child murder's
on the rise. A fly grazes the dog's hide,
which shivers. Primitive brain surgery
involved poking a hole in the sufferer's
skull, a cranial skylight through which
blinding pain or hallucinations
could escape. Sometimes it worked.
Flatworms just grow new heads when needed.
I wear my learned helplessness pinned
to my blouse like a spider's egg sac,
in lieu of your corsage. Brush against me
and it'll rupture, spilling pale
pollenlike spiders. Elephants
ransacked the hunters' tent,
removed a pile of ivory tusks
and buried them. Fascinating to be yanked
out of bed by strange hands.

Vultures can fly ninety miles per hour.
He pulled the quilt tighter
around him, mistaking its stripes
for protective coloring. Male
butterflies and moths can smell
females miles away. *For Christ's sake,
it was just a love bite.* Sponges
may follow the shapes of rocks
over which they grow. You can't
receive medical attention
at this facility. If a rabbit warren
becomes too crowded, pregnant rabbits
absorb their fetuses till there's
more room. He wakes each morning
feeling like a sore that won't heal.
Pelicans unite to drive fish
into shallow water where they're
more easily caught. For our sound track,
we thought of using a tape of inmates
gibbering as they defaced gravestones,
dug up and scattered the bones of those
they hated. Imagine that tenacity:
to despise your enemies' skeletons,
savoring rancor toward brittle rods
of calcium. Ranks and classes
are highly developed among insects.
Each time I pay my rent, my hoarse
landlord growls: "My dentist's Jewish.
My lawyer's Jewish. There are so many
of you." The dog lies quietly

by the stove, gnawing a cow's hoof
I have given her. My mother claims
I was born with a tail, cut off
by some shortsighted obstetrician.

DEAD HUNTERS

Poor red-shirted brutes—
to wake and find
their trumpets muffled,
decoys turned flesh and fled,
campsites cold, and that old
turncoat, their own ravenous
marrow, now yearning humbly
to serve as worm bait.
What paradise composes itself
out of the pitch dark of death
for *them*? A skyline of drenched,
rustling pines might please.
But they can't stomp around
with a family of bloody rabbits
dangling from their belts
by the hind legs anymore.
Will these men lie in warm heaps
on God's lap awhile
when they first arrive,
wide-eyed, panting,
being petted and spoken to gently
in a tongue they do not know
while their soft-mouthed
dogs, now winged, circle overhead,
like slobbering helicopters?
Armed for eternity with only
their love of faint roads,
of tramping through honeysuckle
and butterweed, how will they pass
the time? The dead hunters
glug black coffee from a vacuum

bottle and watch dawn explode
into a mass of orange and red feathers
every morning, and the force
of that report knocks them
right off their feet.

DIARY OF A LONELY ANTCATCHER

This has been written in the same waterproof ink
I'd take with me in the zipper pouch
of my backpack to make field notes with
when collecting specimens.

Damselflies, Dragonflies, order Odonata.
Abdomen long and slender. Antennae short
and bristlelike. Mouthparts: chewing.
Metamorphosis: simple. Nymphs robust
with gills in rectum. Breathing is accomplished
by drawing water into the rectum through the anus,
then expelling it. Locomotion is achieved
in the same way. Thus the insect moves
by "jet" propulsion.

Abridged Curriculum Vitae
(just the highlights)

• leader of the National Alfalfa Weevil investigation team
• editor-in-chief of the *Stinging Insect Review*, Volumes 1–6

ARTICLES

"Butterflies of Montana," "Cave Fauna of Gainesville, Florida,"
"Sand Dunes of Wyoming," "Weeds in General and the Worst
Weeds of Arno County in Particular," "Some Facts About Grass-
hoppers," "Our Feathered Friends of Wisconsin," "Under a Log,"
"Wild or Prickly Lettuce," "A Catalogue of Moths Known to Occur
in Delaware," "Farmer's Friends," "Our Shade Trees," "Supple-
mentary Notes on the Water Beetles of Florida."

We, who take great pleasure
in the psychedelic patterns
on moths' wings and beetles'
porcelain armor, regret
and deplore the decline
of attractive butterflies
along America's highways
and byways.

Quick prayer before sleep:
For this metamorphosis
I am about to undergo,
make me truly grateful.

The average landowner
has no objection
to your collecting insects on his property
if you conduct your studies
with a modicum of decorum.

If the beginner will spend a little time
studying these illustrations
(the lucid descriptions
and forceful, informative drawings
that will come to form his or her
gleanings from this humble journal),
he or she may find even the diary
of a lonely antcatcher
can serve as a sort of lantern,

a battery-powered flashlight
transmitting a wavering but brave
little tunnellike beam of light
through the surrounding darkness
of the underresearched
and the unknown.

As I approached the hive
I heard such a commotion!
It sounded like a whole barracks
of enlisted men busily
unpacking their footlockers,
or a ship at sea breaking up
during a storm.

A weird thrill tickled my lower abdominal
region as, from my hiding place
in the mulberry thicket,
I watched long-tongued bumblebees
fertilize red clover.

The blood of an insect
is usually greenish,
yellowish or colorless.

Insects fly by whirling
their wings so that the tips
describe a vertical figure eight,

or an infinity symbol, in the air.
An enterprising British physicist
proved this by applying a tiny
amount of gold leaf to the ends
of a living wasp's wings,
and then observing the pattern
the glinting metal made in
the sunlight as the wasp hovered.

Compound eyes faceted like diamonds.

False clown beetle, walking stick, stone fly, earwig, leafhopper, web
spinner, lacewing, fishfly, book louse, bark louse, wounded tree
beetle, bristletail, darning needle, ripple bug, pirate bug, assassin
bug, ambush bug, stilt bug, thread-legged bug, burrower, woolly
aphid, wrinkled bark beetle, glowworm. But this is only the
beginning.

Insects are ready, willing guides,
the punctuation in nature's grand plan.
Their tiny struggles
are not so different from our own.
Our only real possessions here on earth
are the children of our brains.
I know this to be true,
having expended my life
as a hairsplitting specialist,
an avid follower of the green-peach aphid,

one who knew and saluted the riverskimmer,
greeted the sweet potato weevil
and fondly noted his comings and goings . . .
devoting my energies solely to obtaining
and sifting the knowledge which constitutes
my freewill offering to the world.

I can hardly wait. A sizable swarm
is approaching, judging by the sound.

GRASS

The grass looks
good enough to eat
this morning, especially
those new patches,
pale succulent shoots.
Relax. This isn't some
new depth I've sunk to.
Au contraire.
I've risen to this,
advanced my status
to that of a mooing
grazing animal, after
years of living
as an underling,
skinning my bony knees
bowing mighty low.
Prior to this promotion
I was the town drunk,
making beautiful to-dos
night after night,
watching accidents
reassemble themselves end-
lessly, winking at me
obscenely, like those nasty
vague constellations.
Sagittarius, a man with
an arrow, indeed. You can't
fool me. Those aren't my
tears wetting the backs
of your hands,
they're dribbles of whiskey,

temporary liquid splendor,
my "A" ticket to millions
of enraged, repetitive
adventures. Some people
have five senses, others
claim a sixth perception.
When I was good and drunk,
cranked or *half in the bag*
as dear old Dad used
to say, I had at least
ten senses! But never
enough hindsight to know
that coming events cast
their shadows before them,
and that you can spy on them:
a peep show of burgeoning
bad luck acted out by puppets,
a drama of fodder and
cud-chewing, this waking dream
in which I'm blessed
with multiple guts
and everything I swallow
keeps jumping, alive
and undigested
from stomach to stomach.

Losing heart

Destiny's darlings, they wandered through the rubble in evening
  clothes; dazed, bruised, holding hands.

She said I could watch them do it if I liked, without being seen.

Forget the crumpled leaves and the sugary snow; separate yourself
  from them. You can't go back there.

The priest spent the day watering the trees outside the rectory; they
  had been dead for some time.

Being drunk at noon seemed to fill him up, make him feel less
  sketchy.

Let's be more specific about what we mean by "punishment."

He eyed his customers and wished they would leave.

I am trying to charge my spiritual batteries, he said, closing
  his eyes and letting his mouth fall open, as though he were
  going to sing.

Why are giant women more frightening than giant men?

You're eating something and a tooth snaps off.

Look on me as a figure of speech you no longer use.

Can't you hear me calling?

DEAR RAGE MANAGEMENT SUPERVISOR,

The worst part is:
We don't even own
our thinning skins,
this mortal inventory
of splitting hair
and a flaky scalp.
One never truly
lays claim to one's
judgments, phobias,
guilty twitches,
carefully nursed
griefs finally ripened
to the curved purple
of Japanese eggplants,
or one's personal quirks—
those hot angry stars
in temperament's chaotic
firmament. Empty-handed,
hollow-hearted,
I must downplay my spite,
soul still springing
leak after leak, resembling
a colander blasted
with buckshot. I know,
I know—*find a bucket
or a sponge. Start bailing.
Keep rowing.* Begging
your pardon, your clemency,
but it's raining today.
Liquid's pouring in faster
than I can dredge it out.

Plus, there's nowhere dry
to kneel. Must I hunker down
on this little plot
of dripping fiddleheads
and edible water lettuce
in order to receive
my next lesson? Eventually,
I might divest myself
of this heavy, much-breathed-on
shell, and allow my path
to be transcribed by
shining trails of slime—
a silver maze even the rain
can't easily wash away.
My thoughts remain backlit
with sporadic flashes
of incriminating pictures,
the flare of my past crimes
so like corpse light,
or foolish fire.

FUGUE

Although covered with engine oil,
he feared he was going nowhere.
My dead arm, he kept complaining,
and my sandpit mouth. Moans also
escaped him about his custard-filled
disengaged brain and cement-block feet.
For a period of time, he forgot
about showering. We can hardly
blame him. Consider his plight. Even
his teeth seemed hairy. Every morning,
on a stopwatch he'd used while
a sprinter in college, he had to time
precisely how long it took him to shave.
Spirits rose and fell all around him.
Limply, he envied their trajectory.
His bursts of erratic laughter
made friends wonder whether
he was about to take a spin around
hysteria's overwaxed dance floor.
Smothered by panic, he became possessed
by the need to father troops of children,
though the only woman available,
Miss Truth Serum, he could not love.
His summer nights were spent reading
about degenerative nerve disease,
contact sports and letting go.
His skin became the color of powdered milk.
He compared himself to a dog who spends
his days chasing the sun across the floor.
Although he spray-painted his face bronze,
he worried no one would mistake him

for a park statue of some long-dead war hero.
Although he dusted his body with cake flour,
he was afraid he'd be unable to rise
to this or any other occasion.

Duet

One of us can't have sex without tasting blood on her tongue.
The other spends recklessly, till we're in the red.
One of us pedals her bike through the pasture at top speed to
    let off steam, frightening the livestock.
The other lacks both moral courage and grooming skills, so her
    hair sticks up like spokes.
One of us is waiting for someone to topple out of love with her.
The other wants to make people grit their teeth and see stars.
One of us keeps rubbing her finger over her lips, a mild-
    mannered masturbation.
The other shuffles around the house in bedroom slippers, a
    thermometer poked into her grin.
One of us thinks it's best to gauge social issues by considering
    them from the perspective of the dead.
The other was lying in bed doing relaxation exercises when the
    garage exploded.
One of us has a tin ear.
The other has the emotional range of a crow.
One of us dislikes being seen.
The other works shelving books in an engineering library.
One of us is convinced she's breaking down into tiny, highly
    charged magnetic shards.
The other likes to leave the garbage disposal running because she
    finds the grinding such a comfort.
One of us once collected several thousand pounds of rose petals.
The other considers leaving the house tantamount to stepping into
    a social blast furnace.
One of us is a displaced homemaker.
The other is fond of saying, "Someone's going to get hurt around
    here."
One of us has a very sensitive gag reflex.

The other trained herself not to choke, no matter what she had to gulp down.

One of us has mixed feelings about the spirit of inquiry.

The other is weighed down by blunt and sagging griefs.

One of us kicks spasmodically and bleats like a lamb in her sleep.

The other says her guiding light causes her infinite discomfort.

One of us has amassed musical instruments from all over the globe, including a percussion device made of llama toenails from Peru.

The other wanted to be a pharmacist, or a *curandera*.

One of us is still talking a blue streak to a door-to-door nightgown salesman who has long since moved on.

The hopes of the other lie immobilized, just like her right hand when Father stabbed a fork through it, pinning it to the dinner table, saying, "How dare you talk to your mother that way!"

QUEEN FOR A DAY

My crown's a well-polished
copper bundt pan.
These emeralds and rubies
all over my low-cut
tomato-colored gown,
which draw the eye away
from my quivering
décolletage, are jewels
of molded Jell-O.
By waving my scepter,
a sterling silver
egg whisk, over an ocean
of my adoring subjects'
heads after having
whipped up a stiff foamy
mixture of fallacy
and good intentions,
then drinking
the concoction
after it cooled,
I impregnated myself—
not with an heir,
but with this marvelous
invention (patent pending)
I moments later gave birth to:
a muzzle that entirely stifles
infants' cries without causing
any danger of suffocation.
Now I reign over a city

where minds ripen in silence.

2:45 P.M. :

After so many years
of knowing in one's soul
one was of royal blood,
I became accustomed
to these silent observers
constantly fluttering beside me—
shoe-tiers, ear wax removers,
and solicitous chambermaids
borne aloft on powdery clouds
of Pan-Cake makeup,
who help me wriggle out
of my longline rubber girdle
at bedtime.

Dusk:

Recently, an alien spacecraft
visited my queendom. Not much
happened. Trees flowered out
of season, all the insects
in the surrounding area
disappeared, streams ran pink,
that sort of thing. I concluded
it had landed with good intent,
as there was no one left
lying dead when it departed.

7:30 P.M:

Delivering a speech
at a ribbon-cutting ceremony
for the new public library,
I noticed a blind man
reading a braille newspaper
with one hand while the
other gripped a rake instead
of a white cane. "Sightless
but studious farmer," I cried,
"I salute your thirst
for current events,"
and blew him my juiciest kiss.

10:46 P.M.:

Tonight I shall
continue to pursue
my queenly duties
until the last minute
of my short-lived rule:
I'll write a novel on thin-
sliced rye bread,
twist into a pretzel
trying to give myself
a pedicure with my teeth,
avoid stimulants
or psychedelics,
briefly enter the mystical
realms through scientific

pursuits and prepare
a complicated midnight
picnic. I may sneeze.
I will dispatch dragnets
into the cobblestoned heart
of the capital but shall
instruct my lieutenants
to leave the drunks,
for whom I cherish
special tenderness, alone.

THE VIRILITY ROOM

Attempts to convey a picture
of this world-famous chamber
are typically made in vain.
We, the humble authors
of this little study,
have reveled before in similar
futilities, like trying
to describe a particular
sadness, or the blue mist
of inspiration hovering guiltily
around the head of a genius—
a gas too deadly for the average
citizen to inhale.
Our mission's impossibility
now well-established, let's
begin with the furnishings. There's
the huge fireplace, its ominous yawn
hemmed in by depressingly splashy
wallpaper. The thinly padded easy
chair will give you sciatica.
Eleven curtains of goat hair
hang in the room, tickling
occupants till they flip over
onto their backs, kick their legs
convulsively and moan for mercy.
This only occurs when said curtains
happen to catch a stray breeze,
fetid and sweet as the prelude
to obscenity, or the exhalations
of onion-eaters. You can sometimes
save yourself from this ignominious

fate by holding your breath
and keeping perfectly still.
The waters of separation drip
nonstop from taps in the sink.
Here, a knight can drop his shining
armor and get down to business;
in a room for spewing euphemism,
a chamber built to contain
floods of tears and helpless
clinging droplets of all flavors.
Here's a niche tastefully decorated,
fit to imprison the Buddha's patience,
as well as the proverbial
parade of clean and unclean
meats. Silver trumpets are blown.
A daring dress is worn just once.
It is not uncommon to feel like
a human pincushion. Copious lint
collects under the bed, witness
to acrobatic spiritual exertion.
Mark our words, model citizen,
between these four walls
no one's ever been reformed
or forgiven—only bent into
uncomfortable positions, as
grass always is by the wind.

DAUGHTER OF EVE

Our eviction notice was one long tumble
out paradise's thirtieth-story window.
Down, down, down, till
an infant's coffin-pillow
broke my fall and I opened my eyes
to find you lying beside me, groaning.
Sleeping idol, never mine,
I would like to be a man, too.
I covet men's sudden crumbling lusts,
their burdens. I tire of being
everyman's prey, a few gentlemen's
medicine chest, the shipwrecked vessel
from which half-drowned seamen
swim ashore, repenting every breath.
The elegant sameness of my days
is never rectified by sight-seeing,
or by practicing my already flawless
penmanship. Sadly, breast-feeding
does not diminish ambition.
I want to traverse the world
of action, not pick my way
across deserts of cross-stitching.
Let's regress. May I have a pep pill,
or sex change, please? *Parts of your body
are disappearing. Others increase in size.
This is only natural. You're maturing
into a lovely eiderdown, so unlike
the flippant little coverlet
you once were. Here's a frilly quilted
square of silk to bite down on
so you don't cry out at the wrong time.*

The heat broke, reeking of tedium.
Man is a most harmonious combustion
of elements. I saw twelve ghosts
before breakfast this morning,
lady apostles, who in their discretion
left behind nothing but this shimmering
afterimage of their iron wills.

THE STRETCHER-BEARERS

Even given infinite full moons,
nights pockmarked with stars,
we'd never find
all those damaged boys,
patch them up,
dribble water on their lips,
and rush them back
to the tent hospital in time.
It was like trying to gather
every last pearl
after a necklace breaks . . .
between smoky yellow explosions,
with the ground going rubbery
every few seconds,
we could only locate
the ones that groaned.
Babbling, we carried them,
ducking between trees rammed
into the ground about
as far apart as coffin nails,
and providing almost as much
cover. Poplars and beeches
escalated into a riot
of irony, quaking with scorn
for us and elongating
till they penetrated
the hymen of the sky
and became too green to see.

Doomsday

The dark that's gathering strength
these days is submissive,
kinky, silken, willing;
stretched taut as a trampoline.
World events rattle by like circus
trains we wave at occasionally,
as striped, horned and spotted
heads poke out their windows.
Feels like I'm wearing a corset,
though I haven't a stitch on.
Burn the place setting I ate from,
OK? and destroy the easy chair
I languished in. Let birds
unravel my lingerie
for nesting materials.
Fingers poised on the piano keys,
I can't think what to play.
A dirge, a fugue?
What, exactly, are *crimes*
against nature? How many
calories are consumed while
lolling in this dimness,
mentally lamenting the lack
of anything to indicate
some faint mirage of right-
mindedness has been sighted
on the horizon? The world
is full of morbid thinkers,
miserable workers and compulsive
doodlers. *Darling,* my mother
used to croon, *you were a happy*

accident, like the discovery
of penicillin. When I sense
the zillions of cells in my body
laboring together, such grand
fatigue sweeps over me.
Once in a blue moon I smell
the future's breath,
that purgatorial whiff
shot through with the scent
of burnt hair, like when sailors
have been drifting at sea
for a long time and suddenly
they see gulls circling
and the ripe composty odor
of land unfurls in the air,
but they've no idea whether
an oasis of breadfruit
and pineapple awaits them
or an enclave of cannibals.

Nerve storm

(The text of the confession appears to be incomplete. It reads:)

She grabbed my shirt cuff and yanked me into the storeroom. We were surrounded by rows and rows of pickled little animals floating in jars, and a sour smell. She shut the door. It was dusty and hot in there. She kissed me. In my mind, I listed everything I was in danger of inhaling. *Sawdust from the unpainted shelving, disintegrated wings from the dried-up insects lying on their backs on the floor, evaporated formaldehyde, the starchy cotton scent of her lab coat (her pink dress hem peeking out discreetly underneath), perfume, pastrami she'd had for lunch, her horsey sweat from a long day's work.* In that order. There are moments when what you see tumbles down around you and shatters at your feet. Fumes rise. There's a smell like gasoline. You hear sounds you recognize from childhood: fluorescent lights buzzing loudly overhead the way they did in school, precipitating a migraine; or hundreds of crickets trilling in your backyard at bedtime, which had the same effect. Your thoughts become fluid, volatile; their aroma fills the room. This is a nerve storm. You haven't suffered one in a long time. "What's wrong?" she said, her even teeth looking pointy and small, like a squirrel's. There was an almost imperceptible echo in the room. I forget what happened next. Maybe I did kill her.

THE ONE FOR ME

The undertaker's son imitates certain birds perfectly.
He resembles a well-made scarecrow.
I feel like I've swallowed rocks when I first catch sight of him.
He has a good head for figures.
He is distant by preference.
He says, "Everybody's in their own world anyway."
He stoops because his height embarrasses him.
We sit on his front lawn, the white pillars rising behind us.
We sometimes lie down on the dry grass.
He muses, "Why am I like this?"
He's very attached to his spaniel.
I have seen him smile only while reading.
He cares for me but objects to the way I dress.
He suffers from vertigo and ringing in his ears.
He says his father goes off on boring diatribes.
We discuss some unusual murders in the news.
I met his mother.
She's the kitchen's prisoner.
He was locked up somewhere, too.
I was the one who discovered him, oh yes . . .
I recognized him long before anyone else did.

Sad women's harvest song

Tea fields,
tobacco fields,
rows and rows
of roses, milked
for sweet oil
to make perfume.
A grain of wheat
plummets
into the earth
with a tiny cry.
It hastens
to wake
all the babies
in our village
who have looked
exactly the same
for generations.
One day, something
in you just puts
its foot down.
The mud is green.
Your apron is full
again. You wait
and wait
for a booming
voice, lifetimes
delayed, admitting
what our swollen
vacated mothers
would wrap in rags
and set outside

for roving wolves.
A chaotic sky
drenches us.
Grasses ripen
and hide bird-skulls
that crush to powder
underfoot,
also obscuring
family histories,
which are not drunk
back into the black
soil as easily. What
keeps us so poor?
Women here are
noted for physical
strength, length
of life, and for
the fact that our
fathers never let
us go. Only a few
manage to escape
each year
over the high
fragile mountains.

Duration

It's a giant shotgun wedding,
a mass marriage of opposites
presided over by an offended
white-haired maestro.
He looks like Stravinsky,
though his nose isn't as big,
nor is his wingspan.
Black-and-white images
with subtitles flicker,
as do my closed eyelids.
(This is a 4 A.M. dream.)
The maestro raises a full goblet.
Pale chipped lettering quakes
beneath his feet and warns
that each drop of wine
may contain a plague:
boils, frogs, darkness.
He dips his pinky in,
licks it and roars with the head
of the trademark lion that begins
a certain studio's movies.
The wedding guests, all
young girls, are snoring.
But there's much to be afraid of
in the maestro's aged face.
He tosses his mane.
No power on earth can dissolve
the luckless unions he fuses,
save the forgiving tinkle
of your silver jewelry
as you try to sneak in

at 4:04 in the morning.
You drop your keys
and curse softly. I clear
my throat, fold my hands
over the pickets of my ribs
and listen as two birds outside
begin to argue from sheer relief.
In a minute I'll catch a glimpse
of your tired outline as you slump
in a chair to remove your shoes.
Then I'll smell fictitious
salt-laden breezes that waft
over honeymooners rowing boats
on Lake Nostalgia—so similar
to the disappointed scent
that always clings to your skin.

MODERN MADONNAS

Our lady of immunology.
Madonna of feline leukemia.
Our lady of unpaid anesthesiologist bills.
Virgin of earthquakes on the fortieth floor.
Our lady of diabetic blindness.
Madonna of drudgery.
Our lady of deadpan.
Our lady of drive-by shootings.
Madonna of laboratory animals.
Virgin of the safety deposit box.
Our lady of the sales pitch.
Heavy-lidded Madonna of thorazine.
Virgin of planetary tensions.
Personal virgin of stainless steel.
Madonna of the iron lung.
Madonna of the stock market.
Our lady of the statewide blackout.
Madonna of radiation sickness.
Madonna of carbon monoxide.
Our lady of genetic mutation.
Virgin of ether.
Madonna of nitroglycerin.
Virgin of medical ethics.
Our lady of instant cremation.
Our lady of concentration camps.
Madonna of poisoned aspirin.
Our lady of the sniper at the elementary school.
Virgin of the dwindling emergency rooms.
Madonna of the negative horizon.
Madonna of technology.

Madonna of the mass media.
Our lady's machine museum.
Virgin of the revelation of identity.
Madonna of the double-blind study.
Our lady of AZT.
Our lady of psychoanalysis.
Virgin of computer-engineered tax evasion.
Madonna of the synchronized sound track.
Madonna of autonomy.
Our lady of Dianetics.
Our lady of the stalled escalator.
Virgin of food irradiation.
Virgin of chemically induced birth defects.
Madonna of the wildcat strike.
Our lady of cigarette advertising.
Our lady of twilight sleep.
Madonna of suits "made by some poor slob in Hong Kong."
Virgin of the extra "Y" chromosome.
Madonna of fossil fuels.
Madonna of gridlock.
Virgin of the complete blood transfusion.
Virgin of sudden infant death syndrome.
Our lady of organ transplants.
Our lady of the power lunch.
Madonna of after-hours clubs.
Virgin of the oil glut.
Our lady of talk radio.
Madonna of the Gallup Poll.
Madonna of Muzak and call-waiting.
Our lady of sexual harassment.

Madonna of the glib interviewer.
Our lady of the temporal lobe.
Madonna of the caste system.
Our lady of unpaid sick leave.
Madonna of infinite echolalia.

CONSOLATION

You gaze out the car window,
bleary-eyed. It's nine A.M.
Shaggy auburn cows graze
chilly fields along the ragged
coast. Mist unrolls around
their knees like rumpled bolts
of tulle. Drugged by fog,
the herd seems unaware of the cold.
Your childhood, a rickety ladder,
can't bear your weight anymore.
Its skinny rungs have busted.
A long line of ancestors
shuffles across your thoughts
like a chain gang, mumbling
useless truisms in time
to the engine hum.
The light has fled from under
your skin, taking refuge
between your eyes, where
a tiny white scar squirms,
spelling out messages letter
by letter. You're being driven
through an indifferent winter
that sags like a tree overburdened
with birds. If grief turned you
into a sycamore . . . better yet,
if the gentleman in question
was struck by lightning—sizzled
to an unidentifiable crisp—
this melancholy would live on,
hollow, unresolved; eventually

reseeding itself, flavoring
the air, disguised as yellow anise
that springs up by the roadside.
It's hailing pea-sized globs.
The highway climbs and veers.
In your mind, a child grinds
her teeth. Cows tuck their legs
up under them. Dazed leaves unfurl,
renounce their shadows. Our past,
little sister, is reduced to ash
every morning, while the earth
is still smoking slightly,
like a black joke. We round
another bend in the road
and this scene, too, this empty
conceit, completely disappears.

WHEN EMPTY OF LIGHT,

transformation can take place,
occasionally. For example,
in the faint oasis after vast
pain. Rude philosopher armed
with a cheerful spirit, nothing
you chew up and spit out dulls
your teeth, not even me. This time
around, I'm the hum you almost
don't hear in the darkened room
you nap in after sexual exertion.
I surround you, but am nothing
you could touch. I might be described
as a vestige or undertone; a ringing
in your fourth, sixth, and eighth
ears . . . the pin a doctor sticks
in the foot sole of your conscience
to test if it's dead yet.

An invalid

My hair fans out
on pillows embroidered
with gray and green ivy.
In this dimmed room
where God has seen fit
to drop me, I make
observations, which
I note down in a small
cloth-bound book.
Sometimes my feet swell.
I don't mind. Amusing
little blood vessels,
delicate as the branches
of a fossil fern,
appear on my ankles.
Sometimes I get hives.
The light that ventures
in, through my two windows,
is possessed of a chronic
eloquence, like the muted
light scrawled across
the floor of some
secret cathedral
waiting to be unmasked
as random splashes
of blasphemy. My knowledge
of spiders and their ways
increases daily, although
one suspended in the corner
closest to the door seems
to have fallen from grace:

she hasn't moved for days.
I fear the worst, though one
of her relatives didn't
flinch for a week, then
produced a glob of eggs
the size of my thumbnail.
The babies emerged almost
transparent. It made me itch
to watch them scatter.

Outdoors, the ever-present
theater of seasons provides
endless antidote to my
cultivated high-mindedness.
Glimpses of nature,
with its comforting
underlying violence,
are mine to enjoy
in a truncated,
overmagnified way.
This afternoon I was
brought bread pudding
with sliced bananas,
on a tin tray
that has painted in its middle
a picture of a lake in Iceland
with an unpronounceable name.
I don't miss the dinner-table
dramas, since I still hear
the highlights from down

the hall. Last night
my younger brother
was banished from
the dining room, almost
as soon as the main
course was served,
for putting a cigarette
out in his mashed potatoes.
Always overstepping his bounds,
he remains my favorite.

I was originally bedridden
with a case of clinically
significant hiccoughs.
My ailments soon multiplied
and became more interesting
as they accumulated.
My medicines are experimental,
highly touted, foul-tasting—
none as hilarious or effective
as opium or ink. The canyon
behind this house is full
of flowering weeds
and eucalyptus trees so
oily if you strike a match
in their vicinity, they'll
explode.

The outside world is terribly
crowded. All that lives

or ever came close competes
for standing room, shouts
to be heard. Even flocks
of the stillborn, bewildered
by an unilluminating demise,
swarm around certain houses
like schools of unpoppable
bubbles. The fruity smells
of infatuation and sorrow
take up a lot of room, too,
as do unspoken complaints,
fish ponds, vegetable plots
and all that animal magnetism
flashing between beings.
Intellectual paralysis,
that bird of prey, swoops
around, conquering scores
of minds at a time. Even
indoors one can lose one's
foothold so easily, while
appliances hum and mind
their own business, quietly
swilling electricity. There's
no niche for me in such profusion.
I need to watch these proceedings
from the neatly shuttered windows
of my controlled environment.
I think my indefinitely prolonged
mysterious illnesses provide
the right approach. To lull
myself to sleep at night,
I close my eyes and begin

by visualizing what's overhead,
and then working my way down.
Planets, stars, clouds,
mountain summits, radio towers
atop skyscrapers, crowns
of the tallest trees, our weather vane,
our roof (which needs reshingling),
my ceiling, my tile floor, the house's
cement-slab foundation, the crust
of the dirt, animal burrows
in the first crumbly layers of soil,
and deeper down (because the best
is always saved for last), *worms*
turning like white screws
in the chocolaty earth.

AUTOBIOGRAPHY

Moments before I was born,
my mother lost all her hair.
I remember everything: the shrill
exclamations of the women
attending her; and how, after my
bumpy ride lasting hours and hours
I simply slithered from her,
slick with blood, my hair
copious enough to compensate
for her sudden molting, my
character already bespattered.
Never, since that day, have I felt
any fear. God almighty, author
of all our disorders, who might
have made me a worm, thrust me
instead into a bedroom warmed
by a roaring fire, with windows
providing views of a private garden
in a remote corner of this overly
fertile country. Immediately,
the midwife sponged me off
and clapped a tiny cap on my head
so I wouldn't catch my death.
A good deal of snow fell
that winter. My distinguishing
features include a trusting gaze,
the fact that one of my legs is
a full inch shorter than its
mate, and a small birthmark
on my right shoulder resembling
a dried cherry. Of course

I was lonely. I was filled
top to toe with pagan imagination.
Assailed by stings and dregs,
it will surprise no one familiar
with the child-rearing practices
of the time if I reveal my half-
clothed spirit was repeatedly broken:
harnessed and saddled, a most
obedient pack animal, till something
in me swooned and had to be carried
home on an improvised litter.
Picture yourself a person who thought
more than lived, who heard
the tempter's voice daily
and mistook it for birdsong.
I believed messages imprinted
on the undersides of the leaves
of certain trees were intended
especially for me. As an adult,
I wage a constant campaign
(so far unsuccessful) to achieve
tender-mindedness. And now,
reader dear, we find ourselves
here, so far from land,
almost nose to nose.
You have seen and touched
my abrasions and mistakes,
the wounds that nearly killed me.
What you know about me now
irrevocably binds us. So step
out of the shadows. Teach me

to keep still. Don't bother
to knock before entering.
Under no circumstances,
unseen companion,
will you be permitted
to keep concealing yourself
from me. This is the hour
not soon to be forgotten.
I'm beside myself with anticipation.
My teeth are chattering
so hard I don't comprehend much
that takes place beyond the pale
circumference of my face.

ABOUT THE AUTHOR

Amy Gerstler is a writer of fiction, poetry and jour-
nalism, who lives in Los Angeles. Her eighth book,
Bitter Angel, was published by North Point Press
(1990), and was awarded a National Book Critics
Circle Award in poetry in 1991. Her previous seven
books include *The True Bride* (Lapis Press, 1986) and
Primitive Man (Hanuman Books, 1987). In 1987 she
was awarded second place in *Mademoiselle* magazine's
fiction contest. Her work has appeared in numerous
magazines and anthologies, including *The Paris Re-
view* and *The Best American Poetry* 1988, 1990 and
1992. Text works of hers have been performed at the
Museum of Contemporary Art in Los Angeles, and
elsewhere. In the fall of 1989, she collaborated on
an installation at the Santa Monica Museum of Art,
and a related artists' book, with visual artist Alexis
Smith, both of which are titled "Past Lives." The
installation traveled to the Josh Baer Gallery in New
York City in December 1990. She has collaborated
with her sister, choreographer Tina Gerstler, and vis-
ual artists Megan Williams and Gail Swanlund. She
contributes monthly reviews to *Artforum* magazine.
Her writing has appeared in catalogs for exhibitions
at the Long Beach Museum of Art, Los Angeles
Contemporary Exhibitions, The Whitney Museum of
American Art, The Los Angeles Museum of Con-
temporary Art, The Fort Wayne Museum of Art (Fort
Wayne, Indiana), and Security Pacific Inc. She has
taught English and creative writing at Otis Art In-
stitute, Art Center College of Design, and UCLA
extension.

penguin poets